A VISIT TO

Egypt

REVISED AND UPDATED

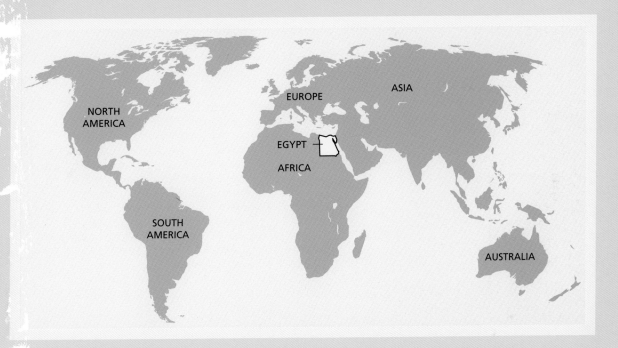

NORTH AMERICA

EUROPE

ASIA

EGYPT

AFRICA

SOUTH AMERICA

AUSTRALIA

Peter and Connie Roop

www.heinemann.co.uk/library

Visit our website to find out more information about Heinemann Library books.

To order:

☎ Phone 44 (0) 1865 888066

📄 Send a fax to 44 (0) 1865 314091

🖥 Visit the Heinemann Bookshop at www.heinemann.co.uk/library to browse our catalogue and order online.

First published in Great Britain by Heinemann Library, Halley Court, Jordan Hill, Oxford OX2 8EJ, part of Pearson Education. Heinemann is a registered trademark of Pearson Education Ltd.

© Pearson Education Ltd 1998, 2008

Editorial: Sarah Shannon
Design: Joanna Hinton-Malivoire
Picture research: Mica Brancic
Production: Duncan Gilbert

Originated by Modern Age
Printed and bound in China by South China Printing Co. Ltd

ISBN 978 0 431087269 (hardback)
12 11 10 09 08
10 9 8 7 6 5 4 3 2 1

ISBN 978 0 431087405 (paperback)
12 11 10 09 08
10 9 8 7 6 5 4 3 2 1

British Library Cataloguing in Publication Data

Roop, Peter
A visit to Egypt. - New ed.
1. Egypt – Social conditions – 1952 – – Juvenile literature
2. Egypt – Geography – Juvenile literature
3. Egypt – Social life and customs – 21st century – Juvenile literature
I.Title II.Roop, Connie III. Egypt
962'.055

Acknowledgements

The publishers would like to thank the following for permission to reproduce photographs: ©Christine Osborne Pictures pp. **7**, **9**, **12**, **18**; ©Getty Images p. **13** (Gallo Images ROOTS RF collection/Russel Wasserfall), p. **29** (Time Life Pictures/Barry Iverson); ©Hutchison Library p. **22**, p. **15** (S Errington), p. **14** (J Hart), p. **28** (Liba), p. **8** (Regent), p. **23** (L Taylor), p. **17** (B Willis);©J Allan Cash p. **20** ©Photolibrary p. **21** (Yvan Travert/Photononstop); ©Robert Harding Picture Library p. **19** (F J Jackson), p. **25** (E Simanor); ©Spectrum Colour Library p. **26**; ©Trip p. **6** (R Cracknell), p. **27** (E James), p. **16** (P Mitchell), p. **11** (A Tovy); ©Zefa p. **5**, p. **10** (C Friere), p. **9** (Maroon).

Cover photograph of columns with hieroglyphs in the Great Hypostyle Hall, Temple of Karnak, Thebes, Egypt reproduced with permission of Robert Harding (Gavin Hellier).

Our thanks to Nick Lapthorn and Clare Lewis for their help in the preparation of this book.

Every effort has been made to contact copyright holders of any material reproduced in this book. Any omissions will be rectified in subsequent printings if notice is given to the publishers.

Contents

Any words appearing in bold, **like this**, are explained in the Glossary.

Egypt

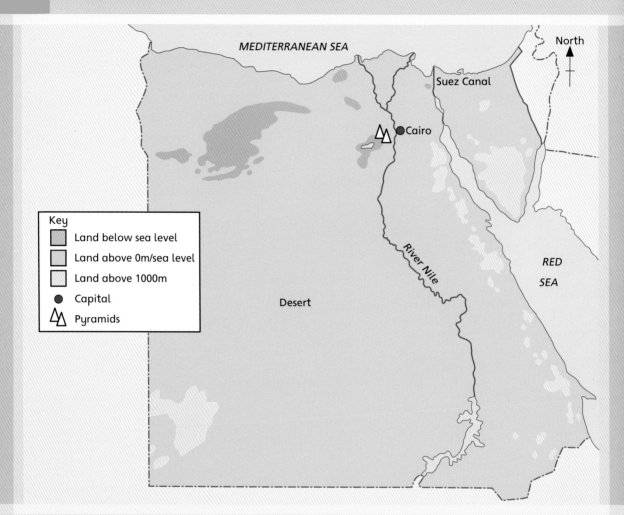

Egypt is in the north-east corner of Africa. The longest river in the world is in Egypt. It is called the River Nile.

Many people visit Egypt to see the **ancient** buildings. More than 4,000 years ago the Egyptians built **temples**, the . **pyramids** and the **Great Sphinx**.

The Great Spinx sits next to the pyramids. It has the head of a human and the body of a lion.

Land

Egypt is a hot, dry country. **Desert** and mountains cover most of Egypt. Not many people live in the desert.

Most Egyptians live along the river Nile. Egyptians have lived by the river for 5,000 years. Today, around nine out of every ten Egyptians still live near the river.

Land by the river Nile is good for growing food.

Landmarks

Cairo is the **capital** of Egypt. It is also the largest city in Egypt and Africa. About 7 million people live in Cairo.

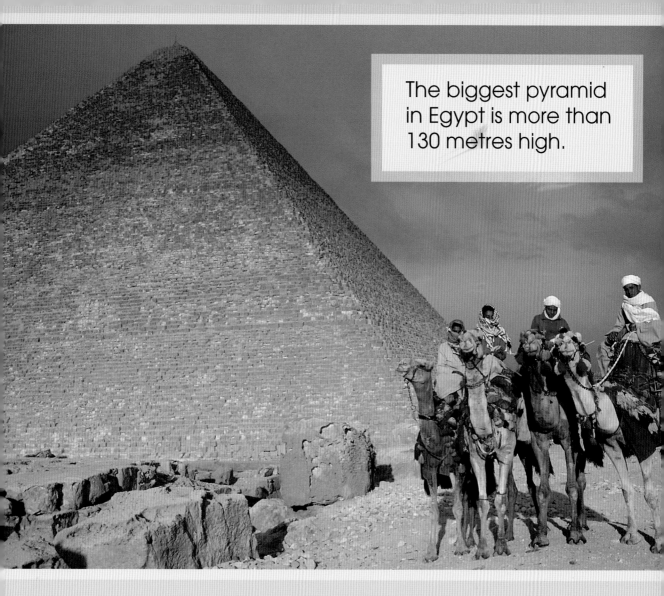

The biggest pyramid in Egypt is more than 130 metres high.

The Egyptians built the **pyramids** for their kings, called pharoahs. They put the body of the dead pharaoh inside the pyramid. They also put in beautiful clothes and jewellery.

Homes

The crowded Egyptian cities have old and new buildings. Most people live in small houses or flats.

In the country, homes are made of sun-dried bricks. The **Bedouin** people live in the **desert**. They live in tents. They move from place to place to find food and water for their animals.

Bedouin people herd animals such as camels, sheep and goats.

Food

Egyptians usually eat five small meals a day. They eat some food on the way to work or school. Food **stalls** sell snacks including rice, lamb and olives.

Baklava are made with pastry, nuts and honey.

Many Egyptians eat ful everyday. Ful is a special mixture of spices, beans and tomatoes. Sweet **pastries** called baklava are a favourite snack.

Clothes

Many Egyptians wear Western clothes. Some Egyptian men like to wear cotton trousers and a long shirt called a galabiyah.

Long sleeves and dresses help keep women cool during the day.

Some Egyptian women wear a black dress called a galabiyah. Many Egyptian women and children dress in bright colours.

Work

Many people are farmers in Egypt. They must water their **crops** often because Egypt is so dry. They grow vegetables, corn, sugar cane, cotton, rice, figs, grapes and dates.

Oil is taken from the ground by machines like this one.

Other people work with cotton, steel and oil **products**. These are important to Egypt because they can be sold to other countries.

17

Transport

Cars are not very common in Egypt. Most people walk or travel by bus or train. They use boats called feluccas on the River Nile.

The Suez Canal is over 100 miles long.

Egypt has a very important channel for ships. Big ships take a short cut through the Suez **Canal**. This saves them from sailing all the way around Africa.

Languages

Egypt's national language is Arabic. People also speak Greek, Italian, English and French.

People sometimes sit and chat in cafés.

Egyptians speak many different kinds of Arabic. Now Egyptians are creating one modern Arabic language. This will help them to understand each other better.

School

All Egyptian children between the ages of 6 and 14 must go to school. Children learn lots of subjects, including maths, science, music, French, English and art.

Most Egyptian schools teach lessons in Arabic but some teach in English.

Egyptian children learn to read and write Arabic. Arabic has 28 letters. You read it from right to left.

Free time

Football (soccer) is a favourite Egyptian sport. The Eyptian football team won the Africa Cup of Nations in 2008. People also play basketball, tennis, **squash** and volleyball.

Egyptians enjoy spending time at the souk. A souk is an outdoor market with lots of **stalls**. They shop and talk with friends and family.

There are lots of things to buy at a souk, such as clothes, jewellery and vegetables.

Celebrations

In Egypt, families celebrate many special occasions together. Weddings are a time for dressing up in best clothes and enjoying good food and dancing.

Ramadan is the most important celebration for **Muslims**. People pray and **fast** for a month. Families get together to celebrate at the end of it.

The Arts

Films are very popular in Egypt. Many Egyptians also like to make music. They play **lutes**, drums and tambourines.

During his life, Naguib Mahfouz wrote more than 30 books.

Egyptians also enjoy reading. In 1988, an Egyptian writer named Naguib Mahfouz won the prize for the world's best writing.

Factfile

Name	The full name of Egypt is the Arab Republic of Egypt.
Capital	The **capital** city is Cairo.
Language	Most Egyptians speak Arabic.
Population	There are more than 80 million people living in Egypt.
Money	Instead of the dollar or the pound, the Egyptians have the Egyptian pound.
Religions	Most Egyptian people believe in **Islam** or Christianity.
Products	Egypt produces lots of oil, cotton, fruits and vegetables.

Words you can learn

ahlan wa sahlan	hello
ma'as salama	goodbye
ismi	My name is
shukran	thank you
aywa	yes
la'	no
waHid	one
itnein	two
talata	three

Glossary

ancient from a long time ago

Bedouin a group of people who live in tents in the desert

canal river dug by people

capital the city where the government is based

crops the plants that farmers grow

desert large areas of land that have little or no rain and very few plants or animals

fast not eating any or some kinds of food for a short time

Great Sphinx the huge stone sculpture built next to the pyramids, it has the body of a lion and the head of a human

Islam the main religion of Egypt

lute a musical instrument like the guitar, played by plucking the strings

Muslims people who believe in the Islamic religion

pastries types of food which are held in a crumbly dough called pastry

products things which are grown, taken from the earth, made by hand or made in a factory

pyramids the enormous stone buildings in the desert that have triangular sides

squash a game played indoors with a racket and a hard ball

stalls tables and shelves laid out with things for sale

temples buildings used as places of worship

Index